Own the Stage

Master the Art of Public Speaking

By Suresh Mansharamani

Contents

Chapters

About the Author

Suresh was born in a refugee camp in Ulhasnagar, Maharashtra. He started his career with a job as an accounts clerk in a garment export house that paid him Rs 300 per month. Further, at the age of twenty-one, with dedication and hard work, he went on to run his own business of apparel export. His first startup!

In 1995, his company introduced one of the most successful IPOs, which was oversubscribed by more than 300 times. This accomplishment won Suresh the Presidential Award. At that time, he had no capital, no education, no mentor, no Internet, no telephone, and most importantly—NO EXCUSES. He became a multimillionaire at the age of thirty-five.

He is now sixty-two years old, but his ambitiousness and "keep moving forward" attitude makes his counterparts feel that he is as young and passionate as a twenty-year-old. He has forty-two years of experience in business and relishes imparting his knowledge to keen entrepreneurs.

Currently, he is on a mission to build India's largest business network: Tajurba Business Network (tajurba.com). His vision is to turn one million SMEs in India into multimillionaires by 2023. This vision and mission stem from his ideology that one should be a job creator instead of a job seeker.

Suresh is a Certified Gallup Strengths Coach, Business Coach, Certified Trainer, Motivational Speaker, and two times TEDx speaker. He is a passionate serial entrepreneur, investor, and mentor. He has helped in laying the blueprint of many businesses and transformed them into money magnets.

Suresh helps people who are engulfed in fear of public speaking and inspires them to become great speakers. He coaches them to be able to speak at Tajurba Talks and TEDx. Not only this, he helps in navigating them to become successful keynote speakers, trainers, and earn a gigantic income throughout their lives. He also organizes **Train the Trainer certification** workshops.

His tailored one-to-one Business Coaching sessions help business owners who want to exponentially grow their sales and profits by ten times in just three to five years and become the next unicorn businesses of India.

Suresh can be contacted at:

suresh.mansharamani@gmail.com

www.sureshmansharamani.com

What Made Me Write This Book?

The stage has captivated me since my childhood. During school days, I participated in various cultural activities.

When I was in college, I won the best debater award and the accolade of the best actor. I won several inter-college competitions. Besides this, I also acted in many Hindi, Sindhi, and Punjabi plays.

Although I had no stage fear even in those days, one thing I lacked was the ability to engage an audience when I was speaking in an arena. I thirsted to learn how to keep an audience engrossed for hours and how to maintain the energy during a full-day training program. This thirst was quenched when I enrolled myself for Train the Trainer certification. It's definitely a worthwhile program that hundreds of people have attended.

It was during that workshop where I learned ways to captivate an audience. I noticed there were a lot of people who, while happy being part of the crowd, would usually succumb to last-minute fright due to stage fear. Thanks to the Baader-Meinhof effect, also called the frequency illusion (the movie *Number 23* is based on a crazier version of this), I started seeing this fear in people everywhere. Friends, family, acquaintances, and even strangers—from accomplished businesspeople to budding entrepreneurs— who seemed confident and happy in one-on-one interaction, turned into blubbering messes of fear when put under a spotlight or anywhere near a podium. As perplexing as that seemed, I realized that anyone could get rid of this fear with the right tools and the right kind of practice. Many of my students, including my wife, have become successful speakers who earlier feared the stage.

It is not just public speaking; your focus should instead be on communication skills in general. You need communication skills to foster various relationships, at work, to win clients and contracts, while aspiring for funds, at Annual General Meetings, press interviews, and so on. And the best part is that it is undoubtedly a learnable skill.

The reason behind writing this book is because I see many people who go up on stage without any practice or preparation and make a fool of themselves in front of the audience. It pains me! It pains me when I am invited to judge a startup pitching session and notice even the best of the startups not getting funded as a result of unimpressive presentation skills.

Primarily, communication is the backbone of our society. It empowers us to build connections, make results-oriented decisions, and transpire change. In the absence of communication skills, success usually stays at distant quarters, and we typically end up blaming our destiny or other people.

Public speaking is one of the essential yet most dreaded forms of communication. Glossophobia, or speech anxiety, is what holds most people ransom. They feel like they have been trapped in a room inhabited by these demons visible only to them as they crawl in closer and closer. It is easy to sidestep such situations during school days. Kids with this fear often find an excuse to be absent when it is their turn to address their class. However, when they grow up, this fear turns into a nightmare as they start missing award-winning opportunities when the fangs of this fear pierce deep into their psyche and hold them back.

This fear of public speaking not only impacts simple, everyday interactions with colleagues, bosses, and clients, but it can have a damaging impact on your career path and your level of success if not handled properly.

Therefore, I felt the urge to help those who think they are not able to live the kind of life they deserve, who believe they do not get ample opportunities, or the ones who do get the breaks but are not able to act upon them. Through this book, I intend to equip you with the tools you need to effectively communicate your thoughts in any and every situation.

My primary focus in life is to positively impact as many lives as I can and help people in discovering their best selves. Throughout this book, I share some real-life Tajurbas (experiences) that can act as a catalyst and turn you into a success magnet. I wish this endeavor of mine proves to be a transformative experience for you!

Preface

Let's begin the book with a quick quiz. How many of these names have you heard of?

Swami Vivekananda	Abraham Lincoln
Martin Luther King	
Dr. A.P.J. Abdul Kalam	Winston Churchill
Brian Tracy	
Robin Sharma	Narendra Modi
Barack Obama	
John F. Kennedy	T. Harv Eker
Steve Jobs	
Zig Ziglar	Oprah Winfrey
Nelson Mandela	

It is highly likely that you are familiar with at least a couple of names on this list. Now, what is the one common denominator among all of these iconic personalities?

They all have been spectacular public speakers!

These are just a handful of names. Sandeep Maheshwari, Dr. Vivek Bindra, Dr. Ujjwal Patni, and many more such personalities have achieved paramount success in just a few years simply because of their public speaking skills.

There have been many such public speakers who have contributed to transforming not only their community or country, but also this entire big blue marble through their impactful speeches. Their life-changing words have transformed countless lives.

Despite this, most of us tend to turn a deaf ear to the significance of public speaking. Now, let us look at it from a different viewpoint. What if I tell you that you employ this form of communication during most of your waking hours? Yes, you read it right.

Upon waking up in the morning, you jump into your jogging suit. While strolling, you come across hands waving at you from a distance, wishing you a good morning. You wave back and stop by for a quick chat. You use your communication skills! Upon reaching the office, you greet your colleagues and boss or juniors. Once again, you employ your communication skills. During office hours, you might come across an irate client or boss or a fiery email. You still respond with your communication skills. After lunch there might even be a presentation lined up where you need to showcase your communication skills to your seniors or prospective clients. Then while returning home, you suddenly remember that you had to buy a bicycle for your kid. You rush to the cycle vendor who is about to pull the shutter. You again put to use your communication skills to not only convince him to hold the shutter for a few minutes but also to charge a discounted price. Upon reaching home, again, you engage yourself in the dinner-table conversation with your family members. After diving into bed, you talk to yourself while labeling the entire day as good, bad, or ugly. This time you use your self-talk skills, which is, again, a form of communication.

"The quality of your life is in direct proportion to the quality of your communication."

— Anthony Robbins

What if I told you that every single day can be surmised as the best day of your life? One best day followed by another even better day! Yes, it is possible, and there is no rocket science behind it. The answer is: By learning the art of public speaking.

Section I

Chapter 1: Why Public Speaking?

A significant part of this question has already been answered in the Preface. Now, let me shine the light on further, yet significant benefits of learning the skill of public speaking.

Public Speaking and Your Job

Helps you in Obtaining the Designation You Deserve

Unfortunately, most employees have been working at a level below their actual abilities. They deserve a better designation, but they still spend the majority of their life working in a job that doesn't provide them ample opportunity to put their skills to good use.

It is how you present yourself at a job interview that ultimately decides whether or not you will obtain a higher-paying job or not. If you can appear confident when you are nervous, you will be the kind of person someone, like your employer, will think of when they have challenging situations arise. By becoming a confident and capable speaker, you instantly put yourself above many others who are not expressive and hence, not impressive.

You are always at your best when you can articulate your thoughts clearly and effectively. And public speaking skills help you correctly accomplish the best of you. After all, the true worth of the knowledge you possess can only be realized when you have the right channel as well as the right way to share your wisdom with the crowd.

Not only does public speaking increase your knowledge during the process of preparation, but it also develops and demonstrates your confidence. Whether you are lined up for a job interview or hoping for a promotion, your spirit is what will make you stand out among other candidates. So, do not shackle your own career; speak up effectively and win the job title that you deserve.

Electrify Your Presentations and Nail Your Board Meetings

The other day, I had the opportunity to counsel a senior manager, David (the name has been changed to maintain anonymity). He expressed his plight of working at the same level for the last six years. Not even his colleagues, but also his juniors, had surpassed him in terms of salary and promotions. Upon further probing, I discovered that although he was a competent manager, he was not up to the mark in one thing: public speaking. Often, beads of sweat would form on his forehead while facing the projector or while addressing his seniors. His hands and legs would start to tremble, and usually, he would find himself falling between the cracks with no signs of recovery. Although the presentations he prepared were some of the best, his nervousness would often jeopardize him, leaving the clients and his seniors doubtful of his capabilities. Eventually, he was reassigned to backend operations.

This drawback troubled him to the extent that he had started to think he wasn't good enough, and so made up his mind to resign from his job. However, before giving up on his career and later on his identity, he took one wise step. He thought of giving it one last try but this time, under the guidance of a mentor, which led to our meeting.

The first thing I shared with him was an incident in the life of Swami Vivekananda. When Swami Vivekananda was just a youth in his mid-twenties, he traveled to the ancient and venerated city of Varanasi, located on the banks of the Ganges River. This was during the years after the passing of his guru, Sri Ramakrishna, and before he went to America in 1893.

Upon his arrival in Varanasi, Swami visited many holy places and met many great scholars of that time. One day, while visiting the Goddess Durga Temple, he was attacked by a troop of monkeys. While he was running away, a monk shouted to him, "Face the brutes!" Vivekananda stopped, he looked boldly at the beasts, and they quickly disappeared.

The incident left a deep impression on Vivekananda and later on in his lectures in the United States; he used it as an example to encourage people to face the dangers of life bravely and not run away from them.

"The ultimate aim," he said, "is not to enjoy life, but to conquer it—to gain a supreme mastery over our own self." This means to gain control over our fears and anxieties, so that no matter what situation we find ourselves in, our mental makeup is so strong that we come out unshaken and victorious.

"Therefore," said Vivekananda, "be bold and fear not. It is fear that is the great cause of misery in this world. It is fear that is the greatest of all superstitions. It is fear that is the cause of our woes, and it is fearlessness alone that brings heaven, even in a moment."

So, the next step was to restore David's shattered confidence through some proven techniques and exercises. I drew a framework and requested him to follow it as a blueprint to vanquish the challenges. After three months, he asked his boss to give him a chance to speak at a presentation where top-notch clients were the audience. The presentation was scheduled for the next week. His boss felt a little apprehensive, but as David had been a diligent employee, he decided to give him the final ten-minute slot. David grabbed this opportunity to regain his confidence as well as gain recognition.

Ultimately, his presentation not only increased the customer base of the company but also won him his lost throne—the tag of Senior Sales Manager. Another eight months passed by and then one day I received a call from him informing me that he had been promoted as the Sales Head.

This story from David's life only shines the light on a small part of how public speaking can equip you with the tools to be a capable broadcaster. You can leave a lasting impression on your seniors with your flawless public speaking skills. This clearly sends a message to the organization that you are a capable and hardworking employee. Next time, when there is a vacancy at the senior level, you may be surprised to see your name on the top of the list of recommended candidates.

Public speaking is a highly-prized skill, whether that be at the podium or in board meetings.

At every Tajurba meeting, we have a nine-minute business presentation by a member. It's a very important day, as the member is given the chance to present his business to all the members and guests. Once, a graphic designer was presenting his business. He was nervous and didn't do his homework well. During the presentation, his PPT didn't work; he fumbled many times. Though he was a great graphic designer, he lost his credibility that day because everyone thought he didn't know his business well. He stopped getting referrals and eventually ended up resigning from Tajurba membership.

Showcase Your Leadership Skills

Public speaking is the best platform to showcase your leadership skills. You might be a good leader, but at the same time, you could be an unsung hero, working at a level that is far below your capabilities. You might have the instinct to influence your colleagues and teammates; you might even have the ability to push the pedal to the metal and showcase your sincerity to your organization. But there could be one thing that might be keeping you at bay; the fear of handling the stage.

Remember, **you cannot be a leader without followers**. The best leaders inspire and persuade people to rally around them and fight for their vision, and you can't do that if you can't communicate well. A leader needs to know how to get his or her ideas across and get people excited about them. So, if you see yourself as a leader of the future, public speaking is a fundamental skill for you.

Public speaking improves your leadership skills and makes you a more deserving candidate to succeed in your chosen field. As Bill Gates once said, "As we look ahead into the next century, leaders will be those who will empower others."

Public Speaking and Your Business

Pitching for Funding that Converts

I have attended many pitching sessions conducted by startups and have seen mediocre startups obtain instant funding because the founder was a great presenter. On the other hand, I have also seen great businesses not receive funding because the founder couldn't present his business very well in front of the investors.

Recently, I came across a businessman who is a millionaire. He has been involved in his chosen field for the last thirty years. Being a millionaire is a proud achievement, but he was not happy. His plight was that he and his uncle's son started at the same time, with the same investment, and the same product. To add to it, both had the same qualifications background. However, his uncle's son was five times richer than this gentleman. Although they were good friends, this huge margin often worried him.

Upon further probing, I found out that his uncle's son was an active participant in the business deals. Rather than his sales manager approaching the clients, he would take the lead himself. He would prepare the presentation slides on his own, which boosted the confidence of his clients; this further boosted the funding and hence the gains. Additionally, he often communicated with his employees and typically handled their problems directly instead of passing the buck to HR or his manger. This made the employees feel valued, and as a result, they were more invested in the organization, which motivated them to go the extra mile for a supervisor who seemed to genuinely care about their needs.

Unlike his cousin, this gentleman was apprehensive of meeting with clients. To mask his reluctance, he said, "If I have to do everything on my own, then why do I need to hire qualified staff?" I said, "This is the difference between your mindset and his mindset, and hence, your profit misses a few zeros." Even though he was aware of this opportunity in the back of his mind, his fear would hold him back. After a few minutes of our session, the first thing he did was enroll in my public speaking session. He smiled and said, "This is something I had been running away from for years, but I think it is now time to take the bull by the horns."

He met me after a couple of months and with an ear-to-ear-smile, he said, "Public speaking does matter! I am not only able to rope in more investors; the work environment has also changed drastically. The employees are now more energetic and hence, more productive. You have revolutionized my business!"

Handle PR Like a Pro

Public speaking imparts a new dimension to your confidence when you are putting your ideas across the table and endorsing your business. Whether those be networking events or leading PR campaigns, public speaking can ensure a smooth sail for you. You do not have to worry about stumbling or landing yourself in the face of challenges. After consistent practice, you can unearth the best ways to express your vision about the company. You won't find yourself knocked down even if you find yourself bombarded by unanticipated questions. You will have the finesse to handle any situation like a pro.

In 1995 when we changed our company structure to Public Limited and listed it on the stock exchange, our merchant banker organized press conferences in all the major cities of India. I had to go through lots of interviews and deliver many speeches at these conferences. The press rated the conferences as good, and very high rating was reported across all the cities of the country. Two primary reasons behind the success were the fundamentals that the company was structured on, and the media admired my presentations.

At the same time, I would like to add here that handling PR to increase your public awareness does not merely involve delivering your sales pitch from across the table or stage. You need to provide something that is of value to your targeted audience, which should not only be educative but also informative. This type of speaking results in several favorable things for you:

- It announces you as an expert in whatever subject you are talking about. You become the resource, and people like to buy from experts.

- When handling PR, you are in a giving mode. You are imparting information, tips, techniques, methods, and ideas. You may even be sharing some stories or real-life experiences that your audience will relate to and learn from. Your audience will appreciate such insights.

- You are cost-effective. Delivering your message once for many to hear is much more useful than providing it many times to every single prospect.

- You develop a relationship by offering a means to communicate with you. Many people will want to talk to you after you speak or follow up with you through one channel or the other.

- You develop a convertible list of highly targeted people to market to after your presentation. These targeted and interested audience members are more likely to buy from you than from someone who has a limited presence. They would like to be connected with someone they have heard rather than someone unknown to them.

Create Growth Opportunities

Unlike being like a frog of the well, you may have the desire to grow and reach new pinnacles. Here, I would say that practice is the key. The more you practice to master this skill, the more likely you are to deliver with persuasion. People admire such leaders who walk their talk with confidence and enthusiasm. This reminds me of iconic personalities like Ratan Tata and Azim Premji. I have come across a lot of Tata and Wipro employees, who love their company and want to retire from the same company rather than switching to other companies offering lucrative packages. They idolize such leaders to the extent that they consider their work as their passion. On the other hand, such exemplary personalities also keep their investors eager to work with them. This not only increases the bandwidth of prospective supporters but also helps in the expansion of the company immensely.

The Power of Your Voice

Speaking is the doorway to fulfill your needs and aspirations. Whether you want to outshine as a businessman, parent, or a coach; public speaking is the super-highway that caters to all your needs at an accelerated pace. Most importantly, you become a catalyst to inspire other people and fill their lives with success and happiness to the brim. Are these achievements not alluring enough for you to master this skill?

Communication is the pathway that can bridge the gap between you and everything you want.

Great leaders have always inspired us by what they say more than what they do.

However, most of us have not yet employed our voice to its fullest impact. You are here not to lead a muffled life but to utilize the full potential of your impactful voice.

Hence, it is time to "discover your own voice."

As a human being, speaking is the escalator that can lead to the fulfillment of your greatest needs and desire manifestation.

Once you discover the power of your voice, you will start to realize the great responsibility that comes with it. **You can build walls, or you can build bridges**; the choice is yours.

Whenever I speak, it is me who is responsible for what I say and the impact my words leave on others. I am accountable for whether my words produce positive thinking and inspire others, or if they fall on deaf ears.

Super leaders take responsibility for the words they speak; hence, their words are impactful. That is what we call as the next level of leadership. Simply put, there should be conviction and responsibility in your words. However, your conviction and convenience don't live on the same block. So, you need to identify what your conviction is as well as the purpose of your life. Do you want to live like a leader or a follower for the rest of your life? Your voice has the power to uplift others. You can offer hope to the hopeless and power to the weak.

Formulate Your Voice to Create Value in the Lives of Others

Our voice can either be a gift to raise people up or a weapon to push them down. It all comes down to choosing to deliver our message in a way that adds value to people's lives. There have been many impactful speakers who have used the power of speech against humanity or to cause destruction. For instance, Hitler used his power of speech to wreak havoc, whereas Nelson Mandela used the same power to fight for the rights of his people in a peaceful, yet impactful way. Today, both of them might be remembered, but what matters is who among both is idolized by the masses.

Therefore, you need to ask yourself: How am I adding value to everyone I meet, even if that person is a waiter in a restaurant or the CEO of a company?

You need to look at everyone without being prejudiced and by being authentic in your voice. This brings us to the next aspect.

Be Authentic in Your Voice

Step back and think about what it would be like to operate from a place where you have nothing to defend, nothing to prove, and nothing to hide.

What would it be like if you were to act from that place today? Primarily, being authentic means marking your presence. It means aligning with the best version of yourself—whether you are in front of one person or one million people, or in the dark of the night when no one is looking. There should be nothing for you to hide, nothing to protect.

The real, person-to-person connection that happens when you speak to someone face-to-face is a powerful stimulator. It affords people the opportunity to see that you have the required knowledge and wisdom; that you really walk your talk; and that you have had great success with the product or service you provide, and are deeply passionate about it. You give them the chance to envision themselves working with you. With this, there is a possibility to generate quality leads rather than relying on channels that come in from other less-personal avenues, such as Facebook or Google ads. Such platforms are significant, however, opportunities brought about from public speaking events simply lay the foundation of deeper relationships at a faster pace.

To accomplish anything in life, there should be a compelling reason behind it, which acts as a catalyst. You will learn all the mechanics of public speaking in the later chapters of this book, but before that, you need to be aware of the fact that it is imperative you become as much of a maestro in public speaking skills as are with breathing.

Now, let's move on to the scope of public speaking as a viable career option.

Chapter 2: Is Public Speaking a Viable Career Option?

What is the "Scope" of Public Speaking?

This is a question I come across almost every day. Most of the public speaking aspirants are apprehensive about considering public speaking as a career option. Most of us are enveloped in myths that an engineer, doctorate, MBA, government job, and so on are what should be considered as legitimate professions—not public speaking. So, let me introduce to you the scope of public speaking!

Let's begin with some facts and figures. According to Forbes, "25% of people actually stay committed to their New Year's resolution after 30 days; however, only 8% can accomplish them." Isn't this statistic astounding? This means that more than 90% of people are looking for a catalyst to stay firm to their resolution. Therefore, you have the opportunity to make a difference in the life of nine out of ten people. Besides, the figures I shared are just regarding the New Year's resolution; we all tend to make resolutions every day. We make choices in every waking moment of life, but most of the time, we fall flat on our face. Therefore, 90% of the world is your market.

Most of us are usually in critic mode. Often, issues like hard work without the desired results/salary, our financial condition, not getting enough time with family, job insecurity, etc., get rooted deep into our minds. Well, there is a one-stop-solution to all the problems of your life: public speaking. You can make a difference not only in your own life, but in the lives of those you speak to. You have the option to obtain those gigantic accomplishments that were not even a part of your bucket list. You have the option to "live the life where the world is your oyster!"

Well, this was a glimpse of the so-called "scope." Let's move on to why you would like to become a public speaker.

Why Would You Like to Become a Public Speaker?

We all aspire to become millionaires "someday." We keep wrestling with the daily grind of life and one day die with many unfulfilled dreams. Despite all the hard work, most people spend their entire time leading a mediocre life. Is this what we deserve? Are we destined to live such a suffocating life?

The answer is NO. We all have an opportunity to live a life of abundance; the only thing that gets in the way of living an abundant life is the choices we make for ourselves. Most of us are programmed to live a secure life so we follow what others have been doing. This mindset is what drags us into the rat race. In other words, we choose to be a follower and not the leader.

If you look at the most influential personalities, there is one thing they all have in common: they all have been captivating public speakers. For example, Mahatma Gandhi could inspire millions by addressing large gatherings across India when there was no television or Internet. It is their words that resonate with us even today, inspiring us. Therefore, it is now time for you to switch lanes. Public speaking may not be the only or the easiest way to fulfill your dreams, but it is a sure-shot way to live the life you've always wanted. Public speaking is more of an art and less of a science!

Imagine if all you did was design business cards every single day. Your entire career would be confined to what fits on a small piece of paper. Or if you only created websites for the makeup industry, you would probably notice yourself becoming bored with very similar designs, fonts, and color schemes that attract potential customers.

If you don't challenge yourself to do something new on a regular basis, you lose your ability to think outside the box because you are never stretching yourself as an artist.

"If you don't build your dream, someone will hire you to help build theirs." – Tony Gaskins

So enough of being a follower, it is now time to be a "crowd-pleaser" and inspire a 360-degree change in the life of others!

Now, what follows is the next pronounced question I'm asked much too often, which might have even surfaced in your mind as well.

How Much Income Would I be Able to Make?

It may sound strange to most people that by merely speaking for a few hours, one can earn millions, but it is true. I am talking about the ingress of public speaking in almost all walks of life now. Many corporate companies, government agencies, schools and colleges, seminar companies, trade show conventions and conferences, non-profit organizations, entrepreneurs, and celebrities seek the help of public speakers to infuse confidence in themselves and their employees.

Public speakers present at workshops, seminars, conferences, schools, and many other gatherings. You'll notice these days that former politicians, sports stars, engineers, MBAs, entrepreneurs, and many more professionals branching out into motivational speaking because it's lucrative as well as inspires their listeners.

If you have ever dreamed of being a professional speaker and rolling in money, you would have probably imagined yourself delivering speeches to a crowd of thousands. Right?

So, is this where the big money is? Well, if you measure by earnings per minute spoken—yes! Speakers typically earn between $10,000 and $100,000 for a one-hour lecture. The highest paid professionals are surgeons, but speakers and trainers earn much more than them. The world's most desired speakers command fees even beyond that. It's a very high margin industry. Once your branding is in place and you have some experience, you can also get paid a very handsome amount speaking at a conference as a keynote speaker on the weekends. You can take up public speaking as your extra source of earnings along with your job and after some time you can make it your full-time profession.

Here is how much some of the renowned international and Indian public speakers have been charging lately:

o George Osborne: $85,000 (£66k) per speech

o Sarah Palin: $100,000 (£77k) per speech

o Richard Branson: $100,000 (£77k) per speech

o Rudy Giuliani: $100,000+ (£77k+) per speech

o Hillary Clinton: $250,000 (£195k) per speech

o Arnold Schwarzenegger: $250,000 (£193k) per speech

o Donald Trump: $1.5 million (£1.2m) per speech

Some of the renowned Indian speakers are:

o Shiv Khera

o Ujjwal Patni

o Priya Kumar

o Chetan Bhagat

o Simerjeet Singh

o Yogesh Chabria

All the above earn over one crore rupees from their speaking assignments in just a year.

And believe me, they are not super-human nor are they born with innate skills. You are as capable as they are, trust me!

Now, let's move on to another interesting part: the eligibility criteria.

Trainings & Workshops

There is huge demand for good trainers, as the self-development industry is growing leaps and bounds, currently generating around eight billion dollars. The next step to take after becoming a speaker is to conduct your own trainings and workshops around your specialization.

You can do a Train the Trainer certification and within few years you can conduct your trainings and add value to people's lives.

Eligibility Criteria

Unlike other professions, there is neither a special education degree nor a requirement of former experience as a public speaker.

• All you need is zeal and a positive attitude to assist in the endeavors of different people belonging to wide-ranging sections of society.

• Excellent interpersonal skills and effective communication skills are another important aspect to making a head start in this profession.

• By and large, any personal grooming institute can be deemed as the best place to attain these skills.

Aside from eligibility criteria, there is one requirement that is of utmost importance.

A Compelling Reason

Every goal you set in life should be backed by a compelling reason. Thomas Edison, who was told that he was too stupid, had a compelling reason to enlighten this world and ultimately "there was light." J.K. Rowling had a compelling reason to rise above failure; hence, *Harry Potter* rocked the entire world. Steve Jobs had a compelling reason to revolutionize the technology sector; hence, Apple was introduced to this big blue marble. Bill Gates had a compelling reason to open the gateway to enhanced Internet applications; hence, Microsoft was brought to life, making the thirty-one-year-old the world's youngest self-made billionaire. Abraham Lincoln and Nelson Mandela had compelling reasons for serving the people of their country, and hence, they became the leaders of their respective countries. A person being fired from a newspaper for "lacking originality and having no creative ideas of his own" had a compelling reason to become a cartoonist; hence, Walt Disney was introduced to the world as one of the best-known motion picture producers. Every single successful person had a compelling reason before they made remarkable contributions to the world. What is your compelling reason?

In addition to gauging your compelling reason, you should be goal-oriented. Visualize the specific goal that you want to achieve by giving speeches.

Let me conclude this chapter with a short yet insightful story.

Once, a little boy, while returning from school, came across a vegetable hawker who was paddling his cart across the streets. That day, it seemed like the sun was set on evaporating every single drop of water lying bare on the land. The shirt of the vegetable vendor was completely drenched in sweat as if he had secreted gallons of fluid while towing his vegetable cart. His lips seemed as parched as a desert, but the way to quench his thirst was nowhere in sight.

The boy noticed the paddler's cotton-mouthed condition while he was wiping beads of sweat from his face. The boy walked to the vegetable vendor and said, "My house is just a few steps away, you can come and drink some water." Thinking that the boy might get scolded by his parents for inviting a stranger, the vegetable vendor flashed a tight smile to the boy. The hawker uttered a "thank you" and again started pushing the cart. Suddenly the sound of a gush of water pierced the vegetable man's eardrums. *Is it a mirage?* wondered the bone-dry man. As he turned back, he noticed a water bottle resting on the pile of vegetables. It looked like one of those fancy bottles that students carry to school. Soon the man realized that the little school kid had left the bottle for him to slake his thirst. The hawker's eyes started to scan the deserted street for the boy, but he had already vanished. With a thin film of tears in his eyes, the hawker uncapped the bottle and gulped down the water while saying a blessing for that boy.

What's the moral of the story?

Always leave some of you to help others!

Since we have already learned the importance and limitless scope of public speaking in life, we'll move on to the next section that talks about the *how* of public speaking. Let us learn the nuts and bolts of public speaking.

Section II

Chapter 3: Finding Your Niche

Knowing that public speaking is important is one thing; actually, diving headfirst into it is another aspect entirely. If you are still afraid of public speaking, I promise you won't die! And as Friedrich Nietzsche said, "What doesn't kill you makes you stronger." So, it is time to get on the brass tracks of public speaking.

Discover Your Own Speaking Niche

The first step is to identify your speaking niche. Therefore, you need to evaluate what you are good at and what your industry or field of interest is. This should be something you are not only good at but have some expertise in. Finding your speaking niche is critical in establishing your speaking career. You can't just list everything as your subject matter. As much as you would like to believe that your speaking or training topic will benefit everyone, it is far from the truth. You might have heard the phrase "Jack-of-all-trades; master of none." Most speakers and trainers fall short because they try talking about everything to everyone.

Here, the best approach is NOT to focus on your weaknesses but to work on your strengths.

Once there were two farmers: Tom and Harry. Tom had five acres of land to plow on, whereas Harry received only two acres of land as a legacy from his father. Although they were close friends, Tom would often brag about his expansive fields.

Both fields had certain patches that were not fertile. Where Tom was obsessed about turning all five acres into a productive terra firma, Harry focused just on his fertile part. Tom would often call for monster cranes to dig out the rocks buried under that slice of land—and was seen mending the unproductive part of his land with a shovel. On the other hand, Harry was usually seen plowing on the fertile part and used the unfertile part as a home for his oxen. Tom spent a lot of his time and resources in refurbishing the barren areas of his land, which would distract him from paying attention even to the fertile areas. At the end of the entire year's work, Harry's land produced twice as much as Tom's even though Tom had put in so much hard work.

Why?

Because Tom spent most of the season trying to fix the weaknesses, whereas Harry concentrated on the strengths.

It can be tempting to think that your message will resonate with everyone. But the truth is; a message that's too generic won't leave a big impact on anyone. So, it is a good idea to decide if you are going to speak about sales or if you are going to motivate all business leaders. You need to narrow down your niche. Identify the types of groups who you really want to reach so you can create content that will resonate with them. Now here comes the next question:

What Kind of a Speaker Are You?

Are you known for reaching people's hearts and making them feel something they have never felt before? How about helping people step up and move closer to their goals? Or can you masterfully break complex concepts into smaller parts?

You might be known for a blend of these. Knowing what kind of speaker, you are will help you understand what skill set, you need to create the impact you want. Here are the major niches you can pick from:

1. Informational speaker

2. Motivational speaker

3. Inspirational speaker (inside out)

4. Transformational speaker

Work on what kind of speaker you are. List the skill set you need to strengthen to be the kind of speaker you want to be. Understanding which type of speaker, you are will help diminish insecurities that surface due to constantly comparing yourself with others.

Informational speakers are intellectual teachers that provide information and statistics.

Motivational speakers inspire, arouse, and jumpstart their audience. However, the motivation is temporary, and it requires another jump start after 90 days.

Inspirational speakers work from the inside out. Such speakers may intend to awaken the inner self and transform their audience.

Transformational speakers are committed to breakthroughs and provide information, motivation, and inspiration.

How Do You Identify Your Niche?

Here are three easy steps that can assist you in carving out your niche and choosing the one that works in your favor:

Step 1: Know your signature strengths

We all are born with certain innate talents. There could be times when your friends, colleagues, or juniors might come to you seeking a solution to their problem. In this case, problem-solving is your natural talent. Give yourself some time to think about things you are good at. Dig deep. Recollect the times when you were able to earn the applause of people around you without a lot of effort.

If you were granted a wish to do anything you wanted for the rest of your working life, what would you choose? Granted, it's an overwhelming proposal, but go for it—dream big! And look at things you like to do in your work as well as personal life.

Besides, during the walk of life, we tend to acquire certain talents, knowingly or unknowingly.

There was a boy who often used to carry a chair to the garage and green fields and watch his father playing golf. Though golf was not his innate skill, somehow his brain started to acquire that it. Today, that boy is known as Tiger Woods, one of the highest paid players in the world. Therefore, while pondering over your strengths, also consider the skills you have acquired over time, the ones you are better at compared to others.

Step 2: What talents and skills do you enjoy doing the most?

If your heart and mind are not in the same place, then they will always be in conflict with each other, which signifies that you are in a situation of imbalance. During such scenarios, it feels as if your heart is communicating to the brain, "This seems right for me." But the brain is saying, "No, do this instead—this makes even more sense!"

Step 3: Of those talents and skills you enjoy, what do people need?

Merely being passionate about a particular niche isn't enough. Make sure there is a need for it; otherwise, your work will remain a hobby and never grow into a paying business. You need to discover the riches in the niches.

The right approach for finding the right niche in public speaking isn't about evaluating which niches draw a larger audience and then trying to pick one. It is about discovering the urgent needs people have and then offering them a solution for the fulfillment of such needs.

This is the most important step for any aspiring public speaker. Choose to focus on the urgent needs since a section of people are literally waiting for someone like you to come along and help them. The audience is more likely to choose a better-regarded and better-informed professional rather than someone offering stereotypical solutions.

You need to evaluate how you can sweep the audience off their feet when you share your wisdom, how you can make a difference in the lives of others by talking about the subject. Remember, impactful speeches are like potato chips. You cannot stop at just one. You need more and more until your fingers do not return with more chips from the packet. Once the packet is exhausted, you are tempted to buy another one. Similarly, the niche that you choose should engross the audience, and they should be eager to hear more from you.

Another important aspect to consider here is that people who come to your speaking sessions always seek a return on investment, which is your session or counseling fee. Your audience wants to be assured that attending your session would be worth their time and money.

So, while picking your niche, be honest with yourself.

Answering the above questions shouldn't take you long if you know yourself well. However, even if it takes a little more time, that's fine! It's imperative to spend time identifying what's important to avoid hitting the panic button later.

Here is a list of trending niches, but by no means is this list exhaustive. You can create your own trend by studying the market needs and infusing your creativity:

1. Becoming a Better Leader

2. Innovate! Accelerate! Generate!

3. How IT Will Change Your Industry

4. The New World of Selling

5. Change/Personal Motivation Strategies

6. Creating a Culture of Teamwork

7. Building Exceptional Client Relationships

8. Personal/Business Growth

9. Embracing the Change

10. Personal Development/Personal Excellence

11. Branding

12. Empowerment; both Personal and Business

13. Storytelling for Business

14. Politics/Economy

15. Healthcare and Lifestyle

16. The Art of Goal-Setting and Achieving Them

17. How to Outrun Competition

18. Power of Social Media

19. Future of Financial Services

20. How to Handle PR

21. Employee VS Entrepreneur

22. How to Overcome Procrastination

23. Work-Life Balance

24. How to Stay Motivated Even During Grinding Times

25. Creative Thinking

26. Gripers, Complainers, and Whiners

27. How to Invest Prudently

28. Is the Education System Full-proof or Fool-proof

29. Highest Paying Careers

30. How to Become a World-Class Speaker

Motivational speaking is one of the niches which is booming across the globe as the ideas given by motivational speakers and the habits endorsed by them are definitely helpful in transforming one's life.

It is you who has to decide what you want to be known for. Your topic must not only serve your purpose, but it must get you excited as well. Remember, the audience does not long to listen to yet another generic speaker—rather, they want to learn from someone who is an expert. So, what's your expertise?

You need to own it, position it, and market it to get speaking gigs.

Choose a niche and gather all your focus and diligence around it. When you start off as a speaker, be prepared to speak on the topic you want to be the go-to expert in. Creative people who seek out new experiences are resilient, observant, and are willing to take risks. This unique worldview helps you solve problems for your clients because of your different perspective.

And that's what they pay you for!

Now that you have chosen your niche, it is time to equip yourselves for the stage. Let's learn about the challenges that are likely to surface and how you can overcome them.

Chapter 4: Outrun Stage-Fear and Own the Stage

"According to most studies, people's number one fear is public speaking. Number two is death. Death is number two. Does that sound right? This means to the average person, if you go to a funeral, you're better off in the casket than doing the eulogy." – Jerry Seinfeld

The fear of public speaking, often called stage fright, takes a huge toll on a person's self-confidence and self-esteem. To some people, it is so dreadful they'd rather opt to leave the job or pass up a promotion. Many people around the globe—including pronounced professionals like actors, athletes, musicians, and CEOs—suffer in silent terror. Excellent performers such as Elvis Presley, Meryl Streep, Barbra Streisand, and Sir Laurence Olivier admitted that at one time or another, they experienced stage fright. And since people feel ashamed, they try to keep their fear hidden, even from their spouse, close family members, and friends. This fear often stops people from laying their hands on the crowning achievements they deserve in life.

There was a lawyer who had a severe case of shyness and was very fearful of appearing in the court because of it. In his very first case in India, he had to withdraw the case because he was too nervous in court. But he didn't give up and decided to learn the skill of public speaking. He practiced and conquered the stage fright and became not only a very successful lawyer, but a legend. His name was Mr. M.K. Gandhi.

I compare public speaking with driving a car. First of all, you can't just get into the car and start driving if you've never done so before; you will be very fearful and won't be able to. If you dare to do that without any knowledge it's going to be a disaster. It actually happened with me. My thirteen-year-old son once took my car keys, and along with a friend, attempted to drive the car. He literally hit the seven cars in the neighborhood. Thank God no one was hurt. On the other hand, if you learn from a proper driving school and an instructor is sitting next to you, within a few weeks you'll acquire all the techniques you need and are ready to drive alone on the road. After that, as you practice, you become an expert driver. Public speaking is no different.

Before we get in to the techniques you can utilize to overcome stage fright, let's find out about some common symptoms that are a sign of this fear.

Symptoms

- Shortness of breath and an erratic pulse

- Dryness in mouth and lumps in the throat

- Wobbly legs, hands, lips, and tone

- Dilated pupils

- Cold and sweaty hands

- Nausea and butterflies in the stomach

- Mental blackout

- Not able to break free from imagining worst-case scenarios

- Increased heart rate

- Inability to sleep

These are some of the most significant symptoms. If you notice any (or all) of them when you are addressing a crowd, it means the fear of public speaking has claimed you.

Darwin's Theory on Fight or Flight Syndrome

We humans are hardwired to be concerned about our reputation to the extent that it sidesteps any other concern. Our brain is conditioned in a way that even a small threat to our reputation disturbs us, and we tend to react. Most of the time, the reaction to the probable threat is beyond our control.

To test the same syndrome, Charles Darwin once visited a zoo in London. He walked close to an exhibit of a snake. Since the exhibit was barricaded by thick glass, he put his face close to it, while almost sharing breathing space. During this, he tried to remain calm since the wall of glass was an assurance that he was out of the reach of the venomous fangs. The moment he moved his face to close quarters, the snake tried to attack him. And every time the snake would hiss at him, he found himself jumping back in fright.

Darwin wrote his findings in his diary:

"My will and reason were powerless against the imagination of a danger which had never been experienced."

Darwin surmised that regardless of our reasoning powers, we humans keep reacting according to our primitive instincts. This is what we refer to as the fight-or-flight reaction. It is our physiological response to a perceived threat which triggers us to either find a way out or stay and fight the danger.

Unlike Charles Darwin's adventure, we usually do not come across such venomous or ferocious animals in our daily life, but we do come across threats like situations where our reputation might get soiled, or we fear being rejected. This can, however, result in losing bankable opportunities.

Such situations are petrifying enough to activate a fight-or-flight response. Hence, we experience symptoms like a lump logged in the throat, sweaty palms, butterflies in the stomach, trembling legs, heart beating like a ticking bomb, and so on

In What Way Does Stage Fright Impact Your Brain?

But this is not the end of the story. During such panicked situations, most speakers prefer apologizing to the audience and walking off the stage with a scar left on the mind forever. However, there are some speakers who retaliate and take control of their mind and body. They rule the stage in spite of adversity. This is what makes them a remarkable speaker. It is not about being fearless the entire time, but about outrunning the fears.

And as they say, "a skill can always be learned," so the good news is that public speaking is a learnable skill. You can acquire this skill by following certain proven ways to overcome stage fright.

If there is a success story that can convince you of the untapped potential of fearful speakers, it is the story of Warren Buffett's unbelievably prosperous career.

He was once a college student who was terrified of getting up and saying his name, but decided to conquer his stage fright. He knew that without this skill he would never be able achieve success in life. He enrolled himself in Dale Carnegie's public speaking course and within six weeks he was able to propose to his soon-to-be fiancé Susie. Warren Buffet never looked back after that and has been confidently chairing numerous shareholder meetings, conferences, and press interviews. It wasn't easy but with practice and expert guidance he overcame his stage fright. He still has the Dale Carnegie public speaking certificate displayed in his office, which he received on January 13, 1952. There is no other earned degree displayed. According to Warren, you have to learn this skill, and the sooner the better. One of the richest men in the world understands very well the importance of public speaking.

How Do You Overcome Stage Fright?

Manage Fear and Anxiety with Communication

The next time you feel paralyzed in front of an audience, remember that you can take fear with you even as you jump and soar. Let fear be the informant on how you can grow stronger with wider wings. Fear is like any other emotion, and it is we who give fear its power. Fear is a made-up story of something that hasn't happened yet, so why not make up a story that empowers you instead?

Harboring a fear of failure is when you really give it permission to fail and not to fly. Not to mention, if you speak with the spirit of ego, agenda, or defending, you are more likely to crash and burn.

Before I introduce and elaborate on the steps to overcome this fear, let me share a short exercise with you to help you take an inventory of the damage fear has done to you so far.

Please write down significant fears and the price you have paid so far for not tackling them head-on:

I am sure the price that you have paid would be an eye-opener to the fact that it is the right time to bell the cat.

But before you begin, I would request you to first ask yourself:

What has fear costed you?

You have paid enough of a price—you are done! You don't go to the grocery store and pay twice, do you? From now on, don't let fear take charge of your destiny.

It's normal to feel afraid or anxious about something that matters to you. However, it is significant as well to take remedial steps when those emotions become paralyzing.

Consider fear as an emotion that informs you to gather more knowledge on a particular subject.

The First Five Minutes

The first five minutes are very important. If you don't have the crowd's energy aligned with you, it won't work. If the mobiles come out, you have lost it. You are nervous. The audience doesn't know you and they don't know what to expect.

If you do the following things within the first one or two minutes, you'll have them with you for the next ten minutes, ten hours, ten days...you get the point!

Here are the few tips to win the crowd in the first five minutes:

1. Start with very high energy. I normally start with a very loud and confident "Good Morning!" My body language reveals my enthusiasm and I always have a broad smile on my face because I feel very happy to be talking to them.

2. Acknowledgements. *Always* acknowledge the organizers and crowd for giving you this opportunity to speak in front of them, and assure them it's going to be worth their time. I always request them to applaud themselves for being present. This invites energy into the room. I also inform them of three benefits of applause: One, it touches your thirty-nine acupressure points, which makes you healthy; two, it brings energy to the room; and three, it motivates the speaker. At this point, the crowd usually gives a huge round of applause. Energy has been built!

3. Ask two Enrolling Questions (EQs) to engage. Now comes the engaging part. Always ask two enrolling questions. For example, "How many of you would like to become TEDx speakers?" Make sure to raise your hand first so the audience knows to raise their hands. Second, "How many of you would like to be paid as speakers?" Most hands will go up. Thank them and move forward. The audience is now fully engaged with you.

4. Earn the Right (ETR). Last, but not least, "Earn the Right." Why should they listen to you? What have you achieved in your life? Ask the audience, "Do I have your permission to share little bit about myself?" After that you can share your life story, achievements, and learnings in about five minutes.

The benefit of starting this way is that it's a very high energy start. Also, once you get the audience to do what you tell them to do, you start to OWN THE STAGE.

3 Steps for Overcoming Fear

Fear is something you have projected in your mind that is going to happen.

If you have projected that I am going to freeze on the stage you are going to freeze. Most people have butterflies, birds, and eagles in their stomach. It has both a physical and emotional impact on you and can be extremely paralyzing.

To overcome fear, anchor three outcomes you want to achieve from your speech.

1. The positive impact you are going to create. Once, I was speaking at a chamber of commerce networking event. After my speech a young man, who couldn't find a job after graduation, walked up to me. He said he was quite depressed because of his unemployment and almost gave up hope of getting a decent job. He said he took lots of notes and was feeling very inspired. I received a very nice WhatsApp message from him. Following is the text message I received from him.

Hi Sir, it's been a long time since our last meet. Things have changed a lot for me. When I met you, I was looking for a job being a fresher (Delhi University) and was hopeless. I kept trying and Got an internship through Letsintern (business development) working in the US market in Sept at an IT startup- FarEye- A logistics Technology company. Got onboarded as permanent employee in Dec earning 6 lacs (around 10000 dollars) per annum as a starting. Thank you for motivating me. I have saved the notes from your talks. This is just a start and I am looking forward to move on to better opportunities. I would love to meet you again :)

Suryansh (Name Changed)

How satisfying it is to making a difference in people's lives with your speech!

2. Three things people are going to gain if you speak. Make a list of three things, three takeaways for everyone, which can add huge value to your audience. It can be your expertise, your unique stories, your learnings.

3. How are the lives of listeners going to be different because they heard your voice? Are they going to be a better spouse, better parents, better citizens?

People will learn how to stand in their power as a result. Women who feel their life is over will know that it's just begun. Men will understand they have the power to press the reset button if they need to.

Replace your fear and anxiety with conviction and clarity. Overcome fear with confidence. Three things you want to anchor on: compassion, viable education, and joy.

Hacking Your Fear

We are talking about bio hacking. How you are going to change your reality. How you are going to control and design it. I think that's wonderful. I did it for a long time.

I had been redesigning my life, always looking at the blueprint called *me* and what works and what doesn't work. Embracing what works and letting go of what didn't work. Some things may be before the season; the season can be six months to six years, and then redesigning it. Not only financially, spiritually, emotionally, and physically. How do you bio-hack the fear?

I had to bio-hack my mindset around money. I had to bio-hack my mindset around my baldness. I had to bio-hack my mindset around my obesity.

I started losing my hairs around thirty-seven years of age. It was quite frustrating and I was unable to accept it. I went to a hair weaving place. They weaved a hair wig with my existing hairs. It was quite painful and the hairs were quite hard. When I woke up the next morning my hairs were standing and I didn't like how I looked in the mirror. I went back to them and complained. They gave me another wig with clips, which was quite comfortable. We went to attend a wedding and I was standing in front of a big pedestal fan and it blew away my wig. Later I learned my personality is what I am inside. People will love and respect you for your character, your honesty, your value, and your ethics—no matter how you look.

I had to bio-hack myself around feeling like a dumb student. I had to bio-hack my complex about speaking English.

There is no miracle that God shows up and *boom!* it all changes. It's going to be the needlepoint move. Next time if the fear rises up, you rise up a little bit higher. Don't make fear your enemy, make it your fuel. Redefine fear because it's an emotion just like any other emotion—such as love and compassion—but we tend to give fear more power. We give it meaning: Fear is **f**alse **e**vidence **a**ppearing **r**eal. Fear is just a story you tell yourself about something that *might* happen in the future. You have zero evidence it's going to happen; however, it's causing visceral feelings within your body. It's time to bio-hack the notion that fear no longer becomes your fortress. Fear becomes your fuel.

Fear will keep you up at night studying, doing more affirmations, leading you to a coach or mentor. Fear is not your enemy, it's your friend. It will remind you that you haven't arrived at the top of the mountain that you are still climbing. Again, fear is your *friend.*

I have achieved the majority of things with some kind of fear inside me. When I began my first startup, I didn't have money for the bus fare. I had to walk 10 km and my shoes had holes. I viewed my shoes riddled with fear.

One time I was traveling on the footrest of the bus and I was beaten by a police constable. I became so fearful and made a promise to myself because I was holding on to the passion. I said, "Suresh, don't worry...I will never be this broke again." Along with my fear and heart full of passion I started to redesign the experience called Suresh Mansharamani.

Are you willing to redesign or level up the design called *you*?

What would you do if you knew you couldn't fail no matter how big you played? If you knew you could survive any heartbreak, any hardship, any breakdown, any betrayal...what would you do? These are all opportunities to become strong; strengthening your resiliency, strengthening your faith. How would the world be a better place to live? Because fear didn't make you stand on the edge. You don't have to wait for the fear to leave. When you are proactive and take action, fear has to dissipate into the nothingness that it always was.

Redesign and reprogram it. You are the designer of your destiny. You are the author of your autobiography. You write the story of your life. No one can write your financial story. No one can write your emotional story but *you*!

The pen has always been in your hand. Write your story that's going to be damn good to read. As you do that you will have to reprogram the fibers of your being. You will have to become someone you have never been, do something you have never done, say something you never said, go places you have never been. You need to redesign yourself, and you are going to be your own Michelangelo, your own MF Hussain. Level up as much as you need to. You are not sentenced to live this life this way. You *choose* it. You are not sentenced to your future. You have an opportunity to change your future.

What do you want? What are you willing to do to get it? If that doesn't make you at least a little afraid, then are you not playing big enough? Your knee is supposed to bruise a little bit, your teeth are supposed to chatter. There should be at least two butterflies in your stomach. If not, you are playing inside your comfort zone, where we mistakenly think we should be 24/7.

Let me tell you something: Comfortability is equal to complacency. I will choose inconvenience every day to make a difference on this planet. I don't mind being inconvenienced if that means I get to leave my footprint on this planet. Confront fear! Get a little angry. Get little pissed.

Your made-up story about the future doesn't exist. Any story you make up is true to you only. Then you live out that story because you want to be right. You don't want to be wrong. And when it comes true you say, "See, I told you guys." You put in so much time and effort to manifest that story. Design a new story. The pen has always been in your hand and no one else can write your story but you.

I want to remind you that my highest grades in school were just 20%, and that my teacher gave me 20% because

I was nice. I was told time and again I was a dumb student and will be a failure in life.

I am not a fast learner but I am a thorough learner. I need to see something several times, I need practice several times, and I need to commit it to memory several times. I am a kinesthetic learner. I struggled all throughout school.

My English teacher said, "You are the weakest student I have ever had in my class."

I wish I could give this book *Own the Stage* to that teacher who called me dumb, and to the English teacher who said I was the weakest student. Some of your fears start to surface because someone said something about you. Some of your best motivation comes wrapped in sand paper. Some of your best motivation didn't come wrapped in love it came wrapped in sandpaper: that nasty divorce, the loss of a loved one, or something that didn't work. Some of the best motivation you needed, some of the best lessons learned, is wrapped in sandpaper.

Your job is to use the opportunity to fuel you, not make you afraid. Look fear in the face. Stand on the edge and hold the fear. Don't wait for it to leave you. Hold fear in one hand, passion in the other, and leap. Because one of three things are going to happen. One, you are going to fly; two, you are going to fall and hit something soft; and three, you have fallen on something hard and need a cast. Remember, you have been built to last. Get up and do it again. Play wholeheartedly. Show up. Become the best version of yourself. No matter what, it's your time *right now* to hold your fear in one hand, passion in the other hand, and take that leap anyway.

I am not perfect. In my imperfection, I am perfect for you. When you become perfect, we can no longer relate to you. So, are you willing to go to the edge and jump? Are you?

Practice, Practice, Practice. There is no shortcut to practicing. Read your speech out loud in the privacy of your room at least fifty times, or maybe more. But nothing beats practicing than doing it in front of a real crowd. Invite a few friends and speak in front of them. Organize your small private event at your office or a nearby community center and practice in front of a real crowd. It may be small before you are ready to face a bigger audience and "Own the stage."

Invest in Yourself. Sign up for a public speaking course at a local Dale Carnegie institute or join a Toast Master club in your area. I also conduct regular "Own the Stage" full-day workshops in Delhi and soon will launch it digitally online.

Add Humor in Your Speech. Be entertaining. Add humor in your speech. Watch lots of videos of stand-up comedians. They are the masters and it's the toughest job to make the audience laugh. Tell your real-life funny stories. When I tell my baldness and wig story, people laugh. Similarly, I tell lots of other stories and actually get made fun of.

Visualize Yourself Delivering a Great Speech. All goals are achieved twice. Once in your mind when you believe you will achieve it, and again when you actually do achieve it. All buildings are made twice. Once in the architect's drawings and the second time in reality when it's constructed. Sportsmen do it all the time. It's called creative visualization. Sit in a quiet place and play some soft meditation music, and visualize yourself giving a great speech. The audience is applauding you and giving you a standing ovation.

Chapter 5: The Basics of Public Speaking: Audience, Body Language and Content

Whether you are presenting to a small group of ten or a large group of a thousand, there are many things you can to do in advance to ensure your presentation achieves the desired response. The most important is to know and understand your audience as well as the venue's logistics.

Know Your Audience

Let's say you are scheduled to deliver a speech on motivation in front of people working at the leadership level. The content of the speech would be different. Whereas, if you have to deliver a speech in front of college students, then your speech is less information-packed and more entertaining. If you have to deliver a speech in front of eminent CEOs, you should prefer content that is more fact-based and informative.

Therefore, it is crucial to know about your audience. Understand their demographics. The people you are going to address is where lays the heart of your speech. You will need to give different messages to different audiences and plan your speech in accordance with various parameters like their ethnicity, age, cultural background, gender, educational standards, social status, their interest area, behavior, attitude, employment, health, and most importantly—what their expectations are from your speech. If you know all of these parameters of your audience, I believe half of the battle is already won.

Know Your Venue

While knowledge of the location of your speech has only marginal benefits for you, the potential pitfalls of not knowing your venue can have a devastating effect on the actual day of your public speaking event.

Let's say you are scheduled to deliver a speech in a different city, which is a metropolitan city. Here, you should know in advance how long it will take to reach the venue. Since metro cities usually witness bottleneck traffic jams, you should consider and leave well in advance. The last thing the audience wants is for you to be late to your own speech. No matter how captivating your speech is, you have already lost their enthusiasm if you arrive late.

Secondly, you should already know if you will be delivering the speech in an open space or in a closed hall/room. You also need to know if you will be addressing people from the dais or through a cordless microphone. If you have the entire stage as your domain, you can use this opportunity to use your body language to make your speech more impactful.

I would suggest to either Google the images of the venue or ask your organizers to share some pictures so you can create a map in your mind.

Body Language

Do you know that only 7% of communication is verbal, while 93% is non-verbal? Yes, 93% is non-verbal! This is comprised of 55% body language and 38% tone of voice.

Your Body Talks

When you hear the speaker, you only hear words. But you feel the speaker only when they have engaged their body. Strengthening your message through appropriate movements is the secret sauce. Communication is like a body sport. *Telling* a story and *projecting* a story are two different things; this is where your body can come to your aid. Throughout the entire process you absolutely need to show people the entire range of emotions by utilizing body language.

You should be aware of your hand movements. Think of yourself as a musician. Your voice is the song, and your body is the instrument. Allow your audience to find their rhythm and perform to your song. Great speakers engage their entire body while they are on the stage.

Using the movement of your body can significantly increase the impact of your speech by 70%.

During a presentation, naturally, legs can be the toughest to control while trying to concentrate on presenting and conveying your message. Jiggling your legs and constantly settling your standing position will signal to the audience that you're uncomfortable and restless.

While presenting, stand confidently and make controlled movements. Your conscious movements should make the audience feel that you have rehearsed these movements before; they should think of you as an expert.

This last area has more variables depending on the specific setup of your presentation. It will be clear straight away on whether you have any flexibility over where you position yourself or if moving around the space is even possible.

For example, if you are delivering your presentation on a big stage, covering a large area of the stage can help create visual interest and keep the audience engaged. Similarly, if your presentation contains engaging elements, you can walk around your audience so they can see you better, which will enable you to feel more connected. However, do not just stay in one area for most of the time because the audience will notice and the ones on the other end would feel neglected.

The golden rule is that every movement should be clear and purposeful—you should never look like you are just wandering around the stage. You may, for example, want to engage your audience early on in your presentation by moving to the front of the stage and asking them a question such as, "Who can tell me..." or "Put your hand up if you have ever..." This not only empowers you to make some judgments about how much your audience already knows about what you have to say, but it also engages them and suggests that you care about their experiences. Most people are happier if they feel a speaker is "talking to" them rather than "talking at" them with no interest in their opinions.

Remember, Your Body Talks!

When you hear the speaker you only hear words. But when you feel the speaker it's because they have engaged the body. Strengthening your message through movement is everything. You have to put your all into your message. Your message is coming from your mind, your message is coming from your tone...you are more than your intellectual being. Your expressions, your thoughts, your passion needs to come through more than what's in your head. Communication is a full-body sport. Showing a story vs telling a story. Point A to Point B. You allow people to experience tangible emotions simply from the movements of your body.

Body Rhythm

When your message is conveyed through your hands, heads are engaged. When, as a speaker, you give all of yourself to your audience, they give all of themselves to you.

You should be aware of your hands. It's like conducting an orchestra, playing a symphony—even dancing. Think of yourself as a musician. Your voice is the song, your body is the instrument. Allowing them to find their rhythm allows them to perform.

Engage your *full* body. Look left. Look right. Move your body. Discover what your mind and body can do together. If you are in front of people and you want their full attention, give them the gift of *all* of you. I can't stress this enough. Using the movement of your body can increase the impact by 70%.

To recap:

- Be aware of your hands when you speak.
- Your voice is the song and your body is the instrument.
- Allow them to find their own rhythm and perform as one.

Create a Dialogue, not a Monologue

How many of you have experienced_____?

Raise your hand if you have ever_____. (Remember to be transparent first.)

Does that concept make sense to you?

Has there been a time in your life that_____?

How many people here know exactly what I mean?

The technique is: echo, repeat, respond.

As you elevate your speaking techniques, create active participation.

A great speech feels like you have been in a conversation. Even if you are talking to 500 people, each one will feel they are having a dialogue with everyone else. When that occurs, trust and loyalty has been given to you, and the relationship happens because you have given them the gift of authenticity and engagement while inspiring their soul.

If you give someone the gift of authenticity, transparency, and engagement while inspiring their soul, they'll go far with you. They will even love you for your mistakes. Dialogue fosters loyalty and trust.

People will have more compassion and faith in you. This is how the audience becomes your waving fan. This is how they are ready to become your students. They become your tribe forever. They raise their families with you. The same happens to your private life. It is about becoming an amazing and profound parent, daughter, son, or father. This technique can be used with 1 or 100 or 1,000 people. A dialogue is an exchange between two people, whether you are speaking to 1 or 1,000. It's all the same.

How many_____?

Raise your hand if_____.

Does that concept_____?

After you ask a question, lead people to respond by nodding. Remember, you are the musician. Keep the symphony going. Keep moving your body.

I don't want you to go through all the mistakes I have made all these years. You can skip over most of those and get right to the good stuff without wasting your time. Whenever you are asking a question, share a bit about yourself on the topic, then ask for responses. But it's not about just you, it's also about *us*. When someone compliments you, say thank you.

Verbal Highlights

How do you grab the attention of the audience without raising your voice?

Slow down your pace. Create rhythm in your speech. Have more conviction and assertiveness. Pause for a few seconds. Find the energy from your core. Lower your voice at times, speaking in a faint whisper. Intensify your speech with spikes in your voice. These tips are only effective for a short period of time. Do it too long and you'll start losing people. When you fluctuate, you create texture.

Whenever I go to my venerable place, I start to whisper. It's like I am sharing a very personal secret, then I show my determination. Whenever I challenge them, I follow that with very a soft tone. Show them you care about them. Your tone should feel like a hug.

Uncover Your Valley Journey

It's the number one way to connect with your audience.

My valley journey post went viral on Facebook. When I posted about my struggles during my first startup in 1978, how I could achieve a 300 times oversubscribed IPO in 1995 starting my career with a job of Rs 300 (five dollars) per month. I was invited for two television interviews and some newspaper coverage.

To be able to connect with others while discussing the lowest point of your life is a big achievement. Share about when you hit rock bottom (if you did), what you learned from your valley journey, why you are so passionate about doing what you do...your *why*. Start with the *big you* by celebrating yourself and your inspiring accomplishments. Differentiating between respect and loyalty.

Mountain-to-mountain and top-to-top is outdated. In between two tops in the valley lives your tribe, your community. Your valley journey has to be relevant. It can be different valleys—finances, relationships, health, obesity, etc. Pick the appropriate relevant valley.

Exercise-how to share your valley journey

1.   Start with *big you* by celebrating yourself and your accomplishments.

2.   Go into your valley, which is an all-time low point of your life.

3.   Share the lessons learned from your valley and why you are so passionate about doing what you do. Your *why*.

The difference between a respected speaker and a speaker who has a relationship with the audience is transparency and vulnerability. To build a relationship, share your lowest points and connect with your tribe.

We all have multiple valley journeys so it is important that the particular valley journeys you share are relevant to your message.

The Pregnant Pause

This is going to make you a master. It's necessary you give pregnant pause. It allows you and your audience to breathe. It allows your listeners to digest what you've said and is an extremely effective tool to use when speaking publicly.

How do you use a pregnant pause?

With fluctuation comes natural pauses. The more you manage to deliver a message with compassion, the more you owe it to your audience. Don't overkill the pregnant pause. Maintain the rhythm. It's a gift to yourself. It's a gift to your audience. Know your audience. I don't do it with financial audiences. But it can be applied in all situations skillfully:

1. The pregnant pause is when you give a statement and then provide the listener with the space to land and breathe before you move on to the next topic.

2. You can use a pregnant pause within verbal highlights following the rhythm and cadence of your voice.

3. It is important to understand your audience so you know how to use the pregnant pause with finesse.

4. A pregnant pause is applicable in any form of communication, from one person to many.

10 Mistakes You Should Be Sidestepping

1. Speaking in Too Low of a Pitch

There are people who brand themselves as soft-spoken who speak in a very low tone. Well, for such people, a microphone is a must. However, speaking softly is recommended but not in a low pitch, so the audience is barely able to catch your mumbled words. Besides, your soft speech should match with your personality. Here, I would largely recommend using voice intonation. Even if you are soft-spoken, you may need to utter things in a commanding voice. I do not recommend delivering the entire speech in an ear-splitting tone and scaring the audience away. Therefore, ensure that you speak clearly and loudly enough to be heard.

2. Using Fillers

Using fillers like "Um," or "Ah'" at some time or another is quite natural. In fact, such fillers bridge the gaps and make the presentation more like a conversation. They can also provide some time to think if you are stuck somewhere. However, excessive use of such fillers can ruin the speech. The audience may feel that you lack confidence or you have not prepared for the speech well. Therefore, avoid excessive use of fillers and keep your presentation jitter-free.

3. Stiff Body Movements

I have seen speakers who even forget to blink while delivering a speech. There have been several politicians who fit into this category as well. Remember, people do not expect to listen to a robot. Stiffness in the body reveals that either you are not confident or you are forced to deliver a speech. Such speeches largely lack the element of connectivity with the audience. So, make body gestures where appropriate.

4. Poor Eye Contact

Usually, people avoid making eye contact even during everyday encounters. However, if you miss maintaining eye contact with your audience, they might feel that your speech is being forced on them. I have noticed speakers who keep looking towards the wall or ceiling during the entire speech. Believe me; words uttered without making eye contact fail to reach the audience's heart. Here, you can mirror-practice by looking in your own eyes. It should not be a stare. Blink your eyes every few seconds. Then you can practice by looking in the eyes of your friends while talking to them. In case you still feel uncomfortable making eye contact with the audience, you can initially try to look at the center of their eyebrows, which is also known as the third eye chakra.

5. Lack of Facial Expressions

Remember, you're not on TV delivering the local news where you just say whatever you have to and go back home. You are there to make an impact on your audience. So, avoid delivering the entire speech with a straight face or by making unusual facial expressions. Your speech will sound monotonous. The best practice would be to synchronize your expressions with your words. Another significant suggestion would be to smile as often as you can. We are so much enveloped in the everyday grind that we have almost forgotten how to smile. When the same people see a smiling face up there on the stage, they feel revived.

6. Poor Organization

A disorganized speech will leave the audience feeling muddled at the end of the speech. Therefore, ensure that your speech has both flow and rhythm. This not only keeps the audience engrossed but also helps you in delivering your message in a fantastic way. No matter how impressive your content is, if it is not organized, it will fail to interest anybody.

7. Low Energy

What is the most important part of the speech when you should be most energized? Is it the opening, closing, or the content part? Well, none of the three. You should be packed with energy throughout the *entire* speech. I have seen speakers who start off with a plethora of energy and seem to continue the rest of the speech halfheartedly. This clearly shows that either you were not prepared or you lost the enthusiasm. Then why would the listeners be interested in the rest of your speech? This is just like a movie with top leading actors in the cast but failing to impress the audience and landing up in the bin. On the other hand, I have noticed speakers with high energy tend to overstate or overstress. The right energy level involves speaking in the correct pitch and pace.

8. Bad Timing

Some speakers address people as if they are chatting with their neighbor. They often make a joke at the wrong time. For instance, you have just shared some alarming statistics with the audience, and suddenly you fire a joke off your canon. Now the information or the data that you shared earlier will not carry any significance because it has been overwritten with the joke. So, here, you need to be smart about how you use the timing in your favor. Smart speakers know when to raise the voice or pause for a few seconds for the information to be soaked up by the audience.

9. Reading (too much) from Notes

This is a mistake most speakers make. To ensure they do not forget anything, they scribble the entire speech and start to read it word for word. Trust me; this does not impress the audience since you miss on many other aspects like eye contact and body movements. Your entire energy is focused on reading the script to the end. This usually results in mobile phones coming out from the pockets. And if the audience has paid for the speech, they won't ever come back to you. Hence, it is advisable to prepare bullet points. Rehearse them a couple of times before "Judgment Day." You may glance at the points once in a while and continue engaging the audience. With PowerPoint presentations, you can ask someone from the audience to volunteer and read on your behalf while you continue elaborating.

10. Using the Stage Area Inappropriately

There have been speakers who tend to either overuse or underuse the stage area. They either move back and forth over the stage or remain stationary. Well, neither of the practices is recommended. Remember, the stage is the opportunity not just to share your knowledge, but what matters more is the way you get your ideas across.

Too much movement can be distracting at times, whereas no movement at all will make the speech dull. I have noticed speakers who, while delivering the speech, step in front of the projector accidentally. The gigantic dark figure on the screen is nothing less than a distraction and a matter of mockery for the listeners. So, be mindful of your steps and the pace at which you walk. Using all the space that faces the audience is recommended so employ them to your advantage.

I understand it's impossible to be completely perfect with these ten key factors I just mentioned. Here, I would like to share a fact: The audience does not want to witness a perfectionist. No one can be perfect. All you can do is get better and better. So, with consistent focus and practice, you can empower yourself to rule the stage. It is not a matter of *not* making mistakes, but bouncing back quickly from your making mistakes so you can learn from them and succeed in the long run.

Content

Opening

When it comes to opening a speech, typical remarks that most speakers make, while warm-hearted, can be a bit boring. They signal to the audience that what they are about to hear is not new, innovative, or even interesting. Even if you are getting ready to share the most incredible information on, let's say, modern technology, you have already hushed your audience into complacency.

Remember, your audience's mind is busy going through their to-do lists and daydreaming as you stroll towards the stage. They have been a victim of dull presentations in the past and wonder if yours will be the same. They are busy evaluating how much consideration to give. How you can captivate them with your ideas in the first few seconds and ease their uncertainty is what matters.

However, if it is left up to you, you might need to list a few carefully selected highlights which can be expressed directly, for example, "I am an MBA from the Indian Institute of Management from Ahmedabad. I have spent the past four years inspiring sales leaders. During this journey, I received a spectacular opportunity to hone my skills."

Your credentials should be weaved in such a way that the audience's initial apprehension is answered—why you.? Also, your opening needs to speak to the audiences about *W.I.I.F.M:* What Is In It For Me?

Finally, you may want to consider *your natural style* while planning an introduction. Here are a few possible ways to start your presentation off on the right foot:

- *Ask a question.* Either one that calls for a direct response, or a rhetorical one. Asking the audience, a question triggers them to start thinking. It's like creating an opening that they want and need to fill.

- *Set high expectations.* At the beginning of the presentation is the key to establishing connection and credibility with your audience. And once you can engage them, your rest of the presentation will go a lot more smoothly.

- *Have an appropriate title to start a speech.* Does your title shine the torch on the vital issue, or is it imprecise? Is the title comprised of keywords that resonate with the audience, or does it only make sense to you? A worthy title is like a trailer to the rest of your presentation.

  For example:

- "It's time to stop being a follower and start becoming a leader."

- "In this session, we will awaken the sleeping giant within you."

- "Today, I am going to share three impactful stories with you."

- **Overview.** Begin your speech by sharing the two, three, or four domains you will talk about, so people know what to expect. The list should not be as long as a grocery list and should not take more than ten seconds.

You may name your domains as your agenda, an outline, or an overview. However, this makes an impact if the list is concise and reveals only the headings of the different things you will be talking about. This allows you to seize your listener's attention and keep them engrossed in your talk.

- ***Be an attention grabber.*** Think of a way to catch hold of your audience's attention when you begin your speech. This could be by putting forth an issue in the form of some questions. Another effective way is by sharing a short story so the audience starts to paint a picture in their mind. You may also share a startling fact at the beginning of your speech. For example, "Did you know, according to a survey conducted by Fidelity Investments, 88% of millionaires are self-made?"

In a nutshell, largely, the audience expects two things from a speaker: a track and a destination. They are eager to know where you want to take them and why. Therefore, it is advisable to mention concisely in your opening what you will be talking about. The simpler and captivating, the better it is. Take out anything unimportant, conflicting, or confusing. Drop off anything that does not aid you in getting your message across to the audience.

Body of the Speech

This is the part that is packed with most of the information. The audience has already been introduced to the subject and the agenda of the speech. Now you need to present your arguments, examples, data, and illustrations that back up your key message.

Nobody likes to feel tied or held hostage by the speaker. Imagine being in the audience. What would be your expectations? Do not make your speech like a wall of text. Make it to-the-point coherent. If they do not understand a blog or a newspaper article, they have the option to read it again. However, they cannot rewind your speech. Therefore, you need to hammer the right nail the first time.

Circumvent sharing abstract or vague ideas. People are keen on actual details. **Do not say**: "There are many millionaires in the world that hold most of the world's wealth." **Instead say**, "According to a Credit Suisse report, there are 2.3 million millionaires who are among 1% of the world's population. And they hold 46% of the world's total wealth."

Please be aware that you are not writing an essay for your school homework. Ensure that any information or data that you share is backed by relevant sources, and the information should sound conversational.

Four Tips to Make the Middle Part Impactful

1. Most people have a short attention span. Therefore, long sentences can fall on deaf ears. Always show a preference for using shorter sentences.
2. Unlike elementary text, use contractions in your speech, or you may sound formal. For example,

instead of "I am" say "I'm," instead of "they will," use "they'll," and so on.
3. Do not opt for tough words when simple ones can work just as effectively, if not better. You do not have to showcase that you know big words and showboat.
4. Never include any jargon or abbreviations in your speech.

What is the most common error most speakers make? They overelaborate or stress on a particular point so pressingly that the audience starts to yawn. There could be times when a specific point requires too much explanation. In such scenarios, ensure that you take relevant pauses and the information should be made interesting. Remember, it is natural that the audience's attention will simmer after a few minutes. They have a lot of other things to think about while you are delivering the speech. Therefore, you must keep the distractions away for them. Don't forget, this is their time, not yours.

So, how can you infuse life even into dull topics? How can you elaborate on a specific point without having the audience lose focus?

Tactics for Engaging a Target Audience

Here are some tricks that have worked for me to help engage an audience.

- **Narrate a story.** We all have a storyteller hidden inside. Recall how passionate you are when you narrate a story to your kid(s), or a group of them. You might have appropriate body language and spiral your tone. Recall the curious eyes of the kids while you are reciting the story. You have to do the same on the stage. Stories are one of the best anchoring techniques you can use to keep your audience engaged. When you narrate a story, the listeners tend to create a mental picture, and hence the wisdom that you offer would leave a lasting impact on their minds.
  If you recall the story of the hare and the tortoise, your mind will immediately associate it with the adage "slow and steady wins the race." You can remember that without even recalling the complete story.

  Personally, I prefer sharing stories from my own experiences, especially about my failures.

IT IS MY IMPERFECTIONS THAT MAKES ME PERFECT

When I share my failures with others, I do not feel even an inch of apprehension since I can harness both my successes and failures as a motivator. When you take the risk of being transparent, the audience pays more attention to you.

Therefore, you can share your real-life experiences in the form of a story. There is no environment where a story doesn't elevate the message. It takes practice to become a master storyteller, and it first starts with showing up.

It's about showing your story vs. telling your story. A visual experience makes listeners feel excited and connected. Anything that you can see comes with more vivid and lucid details.

- **Make it visual.** Using visual aids will always grab more attention than just speaking or relying on text alone. Think about how your information can be enhanced by a diagram or other type of visual aid.

- **Ask questions.** Asking a question, or a few questions, at certain intervals ensures that your audience is actively listening to you. Not only will you fully engage those who respond, but everyone else will be paying attention too. The most relevant time to ask a question is before sharing the next topic. For example, you are about to speak on focus at the workplace. Before you share the next title, you may ask the audience, "How many of you think focus should be the number one priority at work?" The next question can be, "How many of you think that it is okay to sometimes peep across the cubicle to see what your boss is doing?"

Create a Dialogue Not Monologue

- To engage the audience, ask enrolling questions.
- How many of you have experienced_____?
- Raise your hand if you have ever_____. (Remember to be transparent first.)
- Does that concept make sense to you?
- Has there been a time in your life when_____?
- How many people here know exactly what I mean_____?
- The technique is called the echo, repeat, respond.

- **Conduct a poll.** These questions can further take the form of a poll. You can spout off some multiple choice or True/False questions and ask the audience to raise their hands on True or False.

- **Play a game.** You can choose the game according to your message. For instance, your theme is "team-effort," and you have to deliver your speech in a boardroom. You can divide the audience into groups with equal strength. You can give them a task, like arranging the blocks in a sequence or arranging the pieces of a puzzle. This will not only interest them but will also convey what you have to say in a more actionable way.

- **Summarize in a short sentence or use slogans.** This doesn't have to be a fancy one. Many world-class speakers pick a slogan they repeat a few times during the speech. For example, the quote "small strokes fell great oaks" can be said at the beginning of the speech and can be repeated after the above (team-effort) game. Then at the end, you may ask the audience to repeat the quote. This way, they will remember not only the quote but most of the message that you shared after uttering this quote.

- **Play a short video.** Videos are yet another way for your message to resonate in the mind of listeners. YouTube is a wonderful source since you can find several animated or story-based videos related to your topic. Or you can create your own.

- **Surprise them.** Use the surprise element to draw attention. Anything unusual captivates attention. You can share an astonishing fact or show an unusual picture. Some time back, I came across an image of a cat reflecting the image of a lion in the mirror tagged as "Wear Your Attitude.' Such unusual images can leave a lasting impact.

- **Use humor.** Humor tends to lighten the situation. It allows you to gain the audience's attention and build emotional bonding. It can be extremely helpful if your topic is too technical or dull. Your speech may involve sharing too many statistics that are necessary, but the audience might feel bombarded with numbers. In such a situation, you can sprinkle your speech with relevant jokes at certain intervals. But please ensure that you do not throw in canned jokes or the audience may lose interest.

- **Listen.** Remember, you are there not just to speak and bid goodbye. It should be two-way communication. At the end of every topic or every ten minutes, take a pause and ask the audience if they have any questions. Ensure that you an active listener and do not make the audience repeat their questions. In case there is any confusion, you may rephrase, "As I understand, you are asking_____?" In case you do not know the answer to a particular question, you may say, "Well, I am not sure, and I do not want to share incomplete or inaccurate information with you. Please give me some time; let me research and share the answer via email or phone call." And make certain you actually reply to the person. This will make the questioner feel valued and will build the trust factor.

- **Ask for Feedback.** This is, again, a significant part that most of the speakers miss. Before you conclude your speech, ask the audience if they have any feedback. In case someone from the audience shares negative feedback, do not get in a row with the person, or you will ruin the entire effort. If it is positive feedback, you can bow and say thank you. However, if it is negative feedback, accept it politely. After you walk out of the speech room, analyze if the feedback was biased or if this is an area of learning for you. This will help you in getting better and better with every speech.

As you elevate your speaking techniques, create active participation while you talk. To reiterate:

A great speech feels like you are in a conversation. Even if you are talking to 500 people, every single person should feel that you are in a dialogue exclusively with them. When this happens, it hatches trust and loyalty between you and your audience and your relationship with them develops because you have been authentic and engaging while inspiring them with your words.

If you are authentic, transparent, and engaging while speaking before your audience, they are likely to tread far with you. They will even love you for your mistakes and be loyal to you. This is how they are motivated to become your students.

This technique can be used with 1 or 100 or 1,000 people. Dialogue is an exchange between two people, whether you are speaking to 1 or 1,000, it carries the same intensity for every individual.

Another significant factor that I find missing in most speeches is maintaining a balance. Some speakers focus only on information, and some focus only on motivation. If they are highly educated, they prefer showcasing their knowledge, and if they are too eager, they try to become a superhero for their audience. Both these practices are incorrect since these are patterns that the speakers have not been able to break free from.

Inspiration vs. Education - Stir the Soul of Your Audience

Remember words that stick don't land on people's ears, they land in people's hearts. In what way will you speak so that your words awaken something inside of others? It is important to disrupt your backyard and plant new seeds. Abolish old belief systems, old habits, old thoughts, and old behaviors that have proved to be toxic for you. You can educate, and you can inspire. Education delivers the information and inspiration touches the soul of your audience, and so, you must strike a balance between them.

Inspiration awakens something dormant. It will push your boundaries, confront the mediocre, and tap into unspoken desires. It actually disrupts!

Education and inspiration can work in close association with one another, where motivation should be stressed on more. Remember, the human brain cannot store a lot of information in one go. Hence, it is important to infuse education with inspiration in order to leave a lasting impact on your audience.

Chapter 6: **Closing - The Microscopic View**

Too often, we include a lot of content in the opening and the body part, but the ending is usually limited to a "thank you." Such a hurried wrap up suddenly brings the speech to a screeching halt. It seems the speaker's energy has all of a sudden been deflated. Is it not unfair to pour in so much effort in preparing the presentation only to leave the audience remembering your 'fizzle out?" So, before closing, inform the audience that you are about to close your speech. This is so important! It's okay if your closing has a surprise in it, but not if your closing *is* the surprise!

Here are some ways to inform your audience about the closing:

"It's now time to close this presentation."

"I'm going to end my speech with a . . ."

"Let me conclude my speech by . . ."

"My watch is signaling me to close. So, . . ."

Note that the first and last things you say to your audience will be remembered by them for quite some time. This is called "The Law of Primacy (beginning) and Recency (end)." This is why you must have a robust opening and a sturdy closing. Your closing is most likely to be remembered more than any other part of the speech. In other words, your audience is more likely to remember best what you said last. So, ensure you leave your audience with a positive and clear call to action.

Conclude your presentation with boldness, not dullness. Instead of tossing a "thank you," consider sparking off fireworks of the conclusive passionate insights from behind the dice. This will initiate an impulsive ovation to a well-rehearsed, well-executed, and well-timed show.

Section III

Chapter 7: Earning the Right to speak

As mentioned earlier, learning never ceases, but it is important to apply all that you have learned in real life. Here, I have one more significant suggestion for you: Do not wait to become a master orator before you deliver your first speech. That "one day" will never come. Once you have gained confidence in your niche, you can look for a "stage to rage."

Assign a target date by which you will deliver a speech to a large audience. You can break down this goal into shorter goals. Begin by giving a short speech in front of your friends and family members, or in your office. In the beginning, you may want to give a few free speeches to establish your credibility. Once you have the wind beneath your wings, you can look for bigger platforms. There are many professional forums like the Rotary Club, Lions Club, Toastmasters Club, and many more. Besides, each community has its own club like Aggarwal Samaaj Club, Jain International Trade Organization, Rajput Vikas Sansthan, and so on. You can be a part of any of these social organizations.

Start contacting local meet-ups that are looking for speakers and make a name in the local speaker circuit. Network with other panelists and the organizers; often they run or participate in larger events where they screen the speaker applications.

Chapter 8: **How to Get Invited to Speak at TEDx**

First let's get it clear the difference between TED and TEDx.

TED stands for Technology, Entertainment, Design.

TED takes more of a global approach while TEDx focuses on a local community that concentrates on local voices. TEDx stands for "Independently Organized TED Event." TEDx has taken Ted across the planets and thousands of TEDx events are happening around the globe.

TED is about very simplified, authentic storytelling. It fits very well with its TEDx mission of "ideas worth spreading" and is a combination of both. Every TED speaker gets eighteen minutes to speak and sometimes it's the equivalent of a Hollywood blockbuster.

Both TED and TEDx are not-for-profit events. Its staff and organizers don't do it for money, they do it to make a difference. That's why the quality of TED events is very high. TED is about discipline which is why each talk is clean, simple, and extraordinary.

The TED speakers are very carefully curated. The organizers receive hundreds of recommendations and they ask for manuscripts and audio files of speakers. It takes months to prepare for a TED event. Some of the speakers became stars after their TED talks. For example, Amy Cuddy's famous TED talk "Your body language may shape who you are" has around 16 million views on YouTube, and she became a celebrity after that talk. It also helped her launch her books successfully. It's very exciting that someone can get global recognition for an idea they share at TED!

The main TED conference happens annually in Vancouver, Canada, at the Vancouver Convention Centre. Some of its famous speakers include Bill Clinton, Elon Musk, Al Gore, Billy Graham, Richard Dawkins, Sam Harris, Bill Gates, Dolph Lundgren, Bob Weir, Shashi Tharoor, Bono, Larry Page and Sergey Brin, Leana Wen, Pope Francis, and many Nobel Prize winners. In June 2011, TED Talks' combined viewing figure stood at more than 500 million, and by November 2012, TED Talks had been watched over one billion times worldwide (Source-Wikipedia). Over 130 countries and 2,000 cities have hosted a TEDx talk.

How to get invited to speak at TEDx is the number one question people ask me as a two-time TEDx speaker and a public speaking coach. It's the gold standard for any speaker. But to reach TEDx status will not happen overnight. However, it's doable and I personally make sure that I prepare every student of mine for TEDx and recommend them at every local TEDx event. Two of my students were invited to speak at TEDxGSLMC Rajamundry in Andhra Pradesh, India.

It's important to realize that for TEDx you must have an idea worth spreading. That's what TED is looking for. How can it make a difference in people's lives? They are not looking for motivational speeches or self-promotions. Speaking at TEDx creates your authority and make you an expert in your industry.

Start preparing for the journey to TED by following these three tips.

1. *Before speaking at TED*

   If you are not well experienced, I would suggest you start speaking at local conferences as well as either small or big gatherings. Create a YouTube channel and start posting videos at least two times a week. It's okay if you can't get your videos shot by a professional videographer. You can use your phone and learn to use some video editing apps. The same videos can be posted directly on Facebook and LinkedIn. Do not post YouTube links on Facebook and LinkedIn. They don't like people diverting from their platforms to YouTube. Chances are that some TEDx organizer will find you and invite you to speak at TEDx—that's the best situation to be in. I personally followed this route. I never got nominated or recommended.

2. *Get nominated by someone*

The best way to approach TEDx is through nomination or recommendation. Please do not nominate yourself! Someone credible who is an experienced TEDx speaker could increase your chances if they nominate you. You will have to send your topic, manuscript with audio file, and link to your previous videos. Do your research to find a TEDx event which suits your topic because all TEDx events have different themes. Some TEDx events are called *level two* events because they require a higher level of public speaking. TEDx is like the smaller version of TED to get a feel for main TED events, so prepare for that.

3. *Start at a local TEDx*

You can organize your own TEDx event but you can't be a speaker at your own event. The license is valid for one year and it's free. You have to follow the strict guidelines to host a TEDx event. There are different criteria to get the license and are mention at the TED website. Go through all the guidelines before applying for the local TEDx license.

Chapter 9: **Practice is the Key**

Do you know why renowned public speakers can leave a lasting impact on every single speech of theirs? It is because they practice religiously. They follow the quote, "The more you sweat in practice, the less you bleed in war." Every day they follow the schedule of honing their skills, come hell or high water. Even if they take a day off from work, they still do not skip the routine of enhancing their skill every single day.

(Courtesy: https://alyjuma.com/success/) One day, a young man went to the home of Socrates, the great Greek philosopher, and asked, "Sir, I have come to seek your wisdom. Will you help me?"

Socrates looked at the boy and replied, "How can I be of assistance?"

The boy responded, "I want to be a great success. Will you teach me all I need to know so I can be a great success?"

"Certainly, my son," replied Socrates. "Walk with me." Socrates began to walk and headed towards the sea. Once on the sand, Socrates continued to walk straight into the water. The young man followed. When both were chest-deep in the ocean, Socrates placed his hands on the young man's head and quickly forced it under the water. After about ten seconds, the young man fought his way to the surface and began to gasp for air. Socrates released the boy's head, turned, and walked away.

The young man was appalled. He had traveled a great distance to meet with this scholar whom he admired and respected, and when he asked for his wisdom, all he did was put his head underwater. Never again, vowed the young man, would he seek the advice of Socrates.

However, time, as we know, has a way of healing wounds and after a week went by, the young man thought maybe he did something to upset Socrates. So, he went back to visit the scholar. Again, he beseeched Socrates to teach him all he needed to know so he could be a great success.

Socrates smiled and once again agreed. He asked the young man to follow him, and again they walked toward the ocean. Just like before, Socrates walked in the water and, when the water was chest high, Socrates grabbed the young man by his head and pushed him underwater. This time, however, the young man was ready. Before going under, he took a big gulp of air and held his breath for almost for thirty seconds before coming up gasping for air. As he wiped the water from his eyes, he saw Socrates already on the shore walking away.

Now the young man was livid. Twice he had approached Socrates for the knowledge he needed to become a great success, and twice Socrates took him to the ocean and put his head underwater. Never ever again would he be insulted and humiliated like this.

Well, thirty days passed, and the young man had time to reflect. He truly wanted to be a success. Socrates had the wisdom he needed, so he decided to go one final time to see the scholar. Upon arriving at Socrates' home, he rapped on the door. When Socrates appeared, the young man said, "I hope you remember me?"

Socrates flashed a big smile and said, "I do. You are a young man who wants to be a great success."

The young man once again asked Socrates, "Will you please teach me all I need to know and all I need to learn to be a success?"

Socrates nodded and said, "Absolutely." Then he started walking toward the ocean with the young man following in step.

This time the young man was well prepared. As soon as Socrates grabbed his head, he took a deep swallow of air, relaxed, and was able to hold his breath underwater for almost two minutes. When he finally surfaced for air, Socrates had already walked away.

Furious, the young man ran after Socrates. When he was a few feet from Socrates, he shouted, "Socrates, why is it every time I come to you and ask for your help to gain the wisdom and the knowledge on how to be a great success, all you do is take me out in the water and dunk my head?"

Socrates turned around, faced the young man, and said, "Son, I have tried three times now to teach you the secret of being a great success. The secret is simple: **When you want to succeed as much as you want to breathe, you will be a great success.**"

And this is what practice means to successful, yet ambitious orators.

Please follow the following steps to practice your speech

1. Write you speech word for word just as you're going to speak it. Don't leave anything to chance. Write down each and every step. From your first good morning to enrolling questions and ETR. Read that script at least 50 times or more. Speak out loud. Practice voice modulation while reading. You will be surprised how the words come out at the time of actual speech without any fumbling.

2. Practice with bullet points. Annotate bullet points from your speech and speak about each one. This is useful in case you are speaking for few hours or conducting a full day or 3-4 days training. You can take a printout of bullet points and keep it on a music stand to cover all the points during the day.

3. Practice in front of an actual audience. This is a million-dollar tip which I have practiced myself. I would create a small event at some coworking space which is normally free for the organizers and audience. You can practice your speech in front of actual audiences before speaking at the main event. This is the most effective way of practicing and you can shoot your video and watch it later to find areas in need of improvements.

4. Work with a mentor or coach. This is the shortcut to success. If you work with a coach or mentor who had been through all the hurdles and achieved success, it will save you many years of going through the same drill. If you are able to find the right

coach who can hold your hand until you are successful then you will be the luckiest person because technique and Gyan is available on YouTube. You need someone who can believe in you and work with you until you shine as a great presenter, communicator, and speaker.

Chapter 10: How to Get Paid as a Speaker

There is all sorts of advice on how to become a great speaker but no one guides or tells you about how to get paid as a public speaker. Since I have been through that journey, I have listed the following steps to build a business around public speaking. There are no shortcuts to it. You can get paid for one or two gigs here and there but building a sustainable business around it that produces income on a year-to-year basis takes lot of hard work.

1. **Write a book before you speak**. You may be the greatest orator on the planet but you need a book as part of your branding. Without a published author no one is going to take you seriously. It's a shortcut to the stage. You need to keep writing a book every year or at least every two to three years. Keep your ideas fresh and stay relevant to your topic. If you are getting paid to speak you better invest in creating your authority around your topic. Do not have it ghostwritten because if that's the case, let your ghostwriter speak instead of you. These days it's easy to self-publish a book. You can find a good editor at Upwork or another freelance website and get your book edited for grammar and punctuation. It's very easy to publish on Kindle for free. Later you can have your copies printed from the local printer.

2. **Take free speaking assignments**. Before you get paid, work on your personal brand as a speaker. Start posting your videos on YouTube, Facebook, and LinkedIn. In your profile at LinkedIn write *Keynote Speaker*, *Motivational Speaker*, or whatever your specialization is. Chances are that you will start to get invites to speak at local conferences or universities. That's how I started. Speak at local Rotary, Lions club meetings, networking events, LinkedIn Local, etc. There are plenty of events and meetups going on. You will get a chance to practice also when you post your photos and videos on social media. It will help to brand you as a speaker.

3. **Accept a small fee.** After you upgrade from free speaker to fee speaker, initially it's okay to accept the small fee. DO NOT let any offer go just because the fee is small. There will come a time when you will be able to pick and choose, but until then keep accepting whatever comes your way. Make sure you get all events photographed and you must get a video of your talk as well. Do not compromise on that because you may be speaking in front of few hundred people, but later your videos are going to be watched by thousands and millions after you are famous, and these videos are going to make you even more famous.

4. **Master your craft**. If you want to get paid for speaking you have to take it very seriously. Just having expertise in a subject is not enough. You've got to master your body language and your voice

modulation. Also, you need to entertain and add some humor in your talks. Audience and organizers expect an extraordinary experience. You must be highly engaging and energetic. To get paid, referred and, asked to come back again and again requires next-level expertise. You are the show producer, writer, and actor all in one.

5. **Add Value.** Audiences must remember you for a long time after your talk. They must feel inspired and motivated. There should be lot of takeaway for them. As you go from free speaker to fee speaker, think how you are going to add value to your listeners' lives. How are their lives going to change or become better after listening to you? Are they feeling enlightened? Will they share your videos with their network and watch again and again?

6. **Get listed on Speakers Bureaus**. There are plenty of bureaus around. All the corporates or events mangers contact them to book a speaker. Get recommended to these bureaus. If you are branded well on social media they will search and find you. I have never approached any bureaus. They all find me on Google, Facebook and LinkedIn. It takes around two to three years to build that kind of presence and brand on social media before they find you. If you are good there is no looking back after that. Also, they negotiate your fee well,

which you will not be able to do it yourself. They take around a 25% cut but it's worth it.

7. **Build a unique personal brand**. If there is just noise and clutter, why would they invite you to speak? Why are you better than anyone else, or the best in a specific field? Keep reinforcing your brand and uniqueness on social media and with bureaus. Keep posting your videos around your uniqueness on YouTube. You should be posting at least two to three videos every week. Be consistent. Your name should pop up first when any organizer or bureau are looking for someone to speak on the subject you are expert in.

8. **Lifelong commitment to learning**. Never stop learning. These are the three most dangerous words in the English language: I know everything. As a professional speaker keep learning about evolution of new technologies, businesses, economy, and politics. Be informed about new trends and innovations. It will allow you to speak with authority and conviction.

9. **Be ready to face lot of rejection**. Many times, you will get calls for events and even after you confirm a date and agree to a price, you are not chosen. You will never know the reason because they simply don't come back. Be cool about it and once you are empaneled with bureaus, they will deal with it and they will keep getting you assignments

if you are good. They have good relationships with organizers and they trust them.

If you are committed to what I have just described in these nine steps then make a strong commitment to learn everything about polishing your craft and stay on course throughout your life. You may be on the stage for an hour or less but it takes years of commitment to build your brand and track record. But if you stay committed to it the benefits are enormous. There is no greater joy than sharing your knowledge, learning with others, and making a difference in their lives. Be grateful for that because the name, fame, and money will be yours.

Section IV

Chapter 11: How to Organize Your Trainings and Workshops

The real action is when you start to organize your own trainings and workshops. The very first requirement is to identify your topic. Once you identify your topic then you have to do some research if there is a demand for that subject. Do people even want to learn it? You can go to the Amazon bookstore and see if people are buying books about your topic. Check the number of reviews because that will give you an idea.

Also, Google the competition around that topic. You can create your own niche. An example is Marie Kondo. "Tidying Up with Marie Kondo is a reality television series developed for Netflix and released on January 1, 2019. The show follows Marie Kondo, a Japanese organizing consultant and creator of the KonMari method, as she visits families to help them organize and tidy their homes," (Source – Wikipedia). She has found her niche around a very unusual topic-organizing your home. In fact, she has created her own blue ocean and has no competition.

You have found your topic and done your research, so the next thing to do is search your soul. Do you really love the topic? Is it going to make a difference in people's lives? Is it going to be your gift to mankind? Will people pay you to learn that? What will be the outcome if people attend your program?

Last, but not least, be authentic! Don't try to be somebody you are not; it gets magnified. The cheater in you becomes apparent. So, *earn* the trust!

If you get all the three right it's going to be like a hot knife cutting through butter.

It's about the context, not content. Most people think about content. But content is available in abundance on the Internet. It's all about context—who is delivering it and how it is delivered.

How to Set Up the Sitting Arrangements

The most preferable way for the trainings is theater style. Do not use cluster-style sitting. It blocks a lot of space and makes people lazy and comfortable. Buy a music stand and keep your notes on it. Do not ever use a podium; it blocks the energy. Do not use slides. It takes away the attention from you because you'll have to dim the lights on stage, which is worse. If you must use slides to show graphics or videos, use as few as possible. Use flip charts. It's fine. When you write something on the flip chart, stand in front of it so your audience can't see what are you writing. It creates a little bit of suspense and more engagement. Don't be dependent on technology

Music

It's important to have set up your music. Before you start talking, incorporate a little high-energy music. You can invite people to dance to start with fun. I always do that. I enter the hall with very high-energy, loud music, and invite a few volunteers on the stage to dance. It sets the environment. During group exercises, always play soft music.

Chapter 12: How to Get the Audience in the Room and Upsell

I am giving you a million-dollar lesson here. Most trainers don't get it right. They struggle for a long time to fill up the room. Unless you are a big brand, you can't make people pay high ticket prices for your training. You have to make a funnel.

Do the two hours intro program for free. Run the Facebook lead generation campaign and send confirmations to people. Have your office call them for confirmations. Normally at a free program the turnaround is around 60% but that's okay.

Do one-day or three-day programs at a very low cost. Success Resources is the biggest training and seminar company in the world. They do Millionaire Mind Experience (MME), a two-hour program, for free. There, people register for Millionaire Mind Intensive (MMI) at a very low cost. In India they do it at average of 4,000 rupees (around 60 dollars) at a five-star hotel which includes lunch, dinner, and coffee breaks. They get around 800 people in the room. It's a very well-organized seminar with zero error. Once they build the trust and provide lots of value in those three days, they upsell Quantum Leap 5 module programs at around five lacs rupees (8,000 dollars). People line up to buy it. It's easier to sell at MMI because the trust is built. People understand their capabilities to deliver and how it's going to add value to their lives. Before you offer your other programs, make sure to read a few testimonials. The best is having real people giving testimonials. If you can't get real people to come, get their videos.

Once you are set in conducting your trainings, there is no looking back. Your brand is set. You can start to give licenses to other trainers to conduct your trainings. You can deliver your trainings online to the audience across the world. It's the highest margin money-making profession.

Final Note

Congratulations on completing the book! Now your journey to fame and success begins. I conduct full-day workshops on Own the Stage regularly. Please follow me on Facebook and LinkedIn. Subscribed to my YouTube channel. I give away lots of free content every week.

If you have any questions or need guidance, please reach out to me at any time. You may email me at: **suresh.mansharamani@gmail.com**

I believe in you, I love you, and I am your friend in prosperity and possibility.

I wish you all the best!

Acknowledgments

I would like to take this opportunity to thank the Universe as well as everybody who has touched my life. This book is the result of over four decades of experience, learning, practicing, and researching. I was fortunate enough to learn from trainers like Blair Singer, Gulraj Shahpuri, and T. Harv Eker. I thank all of them for every bit of wisdom they have imparted as well as the influence they have had in my life.

My first public speaking experience came from Gulraj Shahpuri, my dear friend who taught me the ABC of public speaking. I completed a Train the Trainer Certification from Blair Singer. I pursued numerous online courses from the T. Harv Eker Academy. I am truly grateful to all my coaches.

I would like to express my gratitude to all my friends, colleagues, Tajurba members, and leadership teams who gave me the opportunity to discuss my ideas with them. The debates and discussions with them helped me immensely in structuring this book. I interviewed numerous Tajurba members; both who had a fear of presentations as well as those of them who are good presenters. They all gave me their insights, which in turn helped me shape this book. I am truly grateful to them.

Last, but not least, I thank my wife Uma, my sons Rahul and Tarun, and my daughter-in-law Deeksha, who have stood by me and have always supported and encouraged me.